Hiding in the Ocean

Patricia Whitehouse

Heinemann Library
Chicago, Illinois

Customer Service 888-454-2279

Visit our website at www.heinemannlibrary.com

Designed by Cherylyn Bredemann
Printed and bound in the United States by Lake Book Manufacturing, Inc.
Photo research by Kathryn Creech

07 06 05 04 03
10 9 8 7 6 5 4 3 2 1

Library of Congress Cataloging-in-Publication Data
Whitehouse, Patricia, 1958-
    Hiding in the ocean / Patricia Whitehouse.
        p. cm. -- (Animal camouflage)
    Summary: Describes life for ocean animals and how they use various types
of camouflage to survive, capture prey, and avoid predators.
    Includes bibliographical references (p.   ) and index.
    ISBN 1-40340-798-3 (HC), 1-40343-189-2 (Pbk)
    1. Marine animals--Juvenile literature. 2 Camouflage
(Biology)--Juvenile literature. [1. Marine animals. 2. Camouflage
(Biology) 3. Animal defenses.] I. Title. II. Series.
QL122.2 .W47 2003
591.47'2--dc21
                                                    2002010283

Acknowledgments
The author and publishers are grateful to the following for permission to reproduce copyright material: p. 4 David Nardini/ Taxi/Getty Images; p. 5 Daniel W. Gotshall/Visuals Unlimited; p. 6 Gerald & Buff Corsi/Visuals Unlimited; p. 7 Gerald and Buff Corsi/California Academy of Sciences; pp. 8, 9 Oxford Scientific Films; p. 10 David Wrobel/Visuals Unlimited; p. 11 Douglas P. Wilson/Frank Lane Picture Agency/Corbis; pp. 12, 27 Norbert Wu/DRK Photo; p. 13 Amos Nachoum/Corbis; p. 14 Brandon D. Cole/Corbis; p. 15 Hal Beral/Corbis; p. 16 MC Chamberlain/DRK Photo; p. 17 Tui De Roy/Minden Pictures; p. 18 Gnadinger/Taxi/Getty Images; pp. 19, 30T Lawson Wood/Corbis; p. 20 Fred Bavendam/Minden Pictures; p. 21 Peter Herring/Image Quest 3-D; pp. 22, 23 Mark Norman; pp. 24, 30B Rudie Kuiter/Oxford Scientific Films; p. 25 Kuell B. Sandved/ Photo Researchers, Inc.; p. 26 Bruce Watkins/Animals Animals; p. 28 Mary Beth Angelo/Photo Researchers, Inc.; p. 29 Kathleen Olson/Monterey Bay Aquarium Foundation.

Cover photography by Lawson Wood/Corbis.

Some words are shown in bold, **like this.** You can find out what they mean by looking in the glossary.

To learn about the manta ray on the cover, turn to page 18.

Contents

Hiding in the Ocean

Many animals live in the ocean. Some ocean animals are hard to see. They use **camouflage** to help them hide.

Some animals hide so they do not get eaten. Others hide from animals they want to catch and eat. There are many ways to hide. This angel shark has **cryptic coloration.**

Hiding on the Ocean Floor

This decorator crab puts **algae,** rocks, and small sea animals onto its shell. That makes it look like the ocean floor.

This decorator crab does not have algae, rocks, and sea animals on its shell. It is easy to see. Other animals can find it and eat it.

Hiding on the Sand

Some animals hide on the sand. This flounder is flat, and it is the same color as the sand. Animals that look like their **habitat** have **cryptic coloration**.

Now the flounder is on sand with different colors. The flounder is easy to see. A **predator** might catch it and eat it.

Hiding in the Water

Jellyfish have **transparent** bodies. They are clear, just like the ocean water. That makes them hard to see.

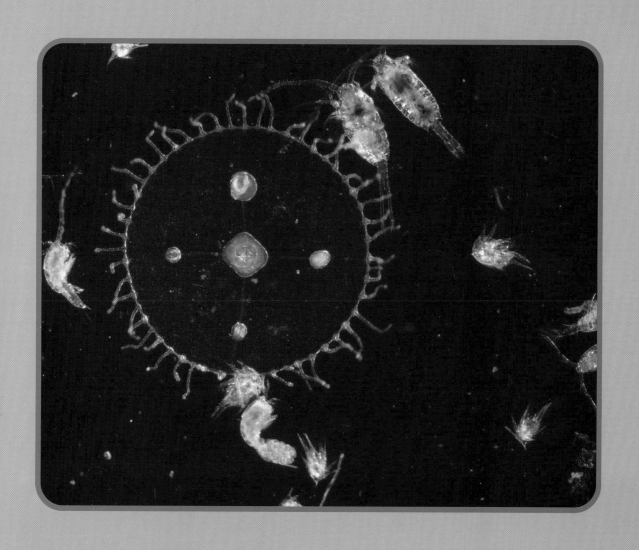

Zooplankton are ocean animals that are too small to see without a **microscope**. Many zooplankton are transparent. Their clear color and small size help them hide.

Hiding by Looking Different

Some animals have color **patterns** that break up their shape. This is called **disruptive coloration.** The zebra bullhead shark has stripes that hide the shape of its body.

An orca's colors break up its shape. Other
ocean animals might only see its white spots.
They might not see the whole orca. This
helps the orca surprise its **prey.**

Hiding to Hunt

Some ocean animals use **mimicry** to hide when they hunt. This stonefish looks like a rock covered with **algae.** It waits and catches fish when they swim past.

This scorpion fish is hunting. If it stays still, other fish will think it is part of the seafloor. They will not notice any danger until it is too late.

Dark Above and Light Below

Some animals have **countershading.** This king penguin's back looks like the dark water below. A **predator** might not see the penguin from above.

King penguins have white bellies. Their bellies look like the light sky above the water. This makes penguins hard to see from below.

Two Colors, One Animal

This manta ray has **countershading**. Its back is a dark color, and its belly is white. This helps it swim and hide at the same time.

A manta ray is hard to see from below. Its white belly looks like sunlight coming through the water. This is how countershading works.

Making Light to Hide

These are flashlight fish. During the day, they are easy to see. Flashlight fish wait until night to hunt.

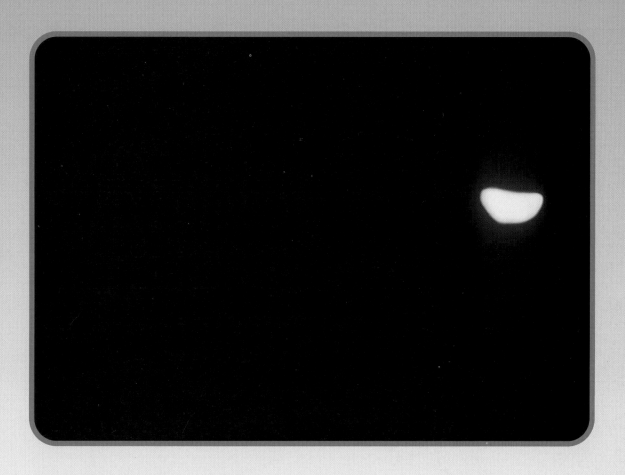

Flashlight fish have a special **organ** that lights up. This light organ makes the fish look strange. The light makes **prey** come closer to the flashlight fish.

Changing Shapes

This looks like a **venomous** sea snake. But it is really a **mimic** octopus. The mimic octopus changes shapes to scare away **predators**.

The octopus has changed its shape again.
Now it looks like a kind of fish called sole.
Many kinds of sole are **poisonous**.

Hiding in Plain Sight

Some ocean animals do not hide. They **mimic** things that **predators** do not eat. This leafy sea dragon uses mimicry to look like a piece of seaweed.

This sea slug hides in seaweed. Predators looking for **prey** will swim right past the sea slug.

Pretending to Be a Plant

This sea **anemone** lives on the ocean floor. Its bright colors make it look like a flower. Fish and other sea animals might think it is a plant.

But the sea anemone is an animal. It waits
until a fish or other sea animal swims by.
Then the anemone uses its **tentacles** to
catch the animal and eat it.

Surprise!

The frogfish looks like a piece of coral. On its head, it has a fake worm. When other fish try to eat the "worm," the frogfish eats them!

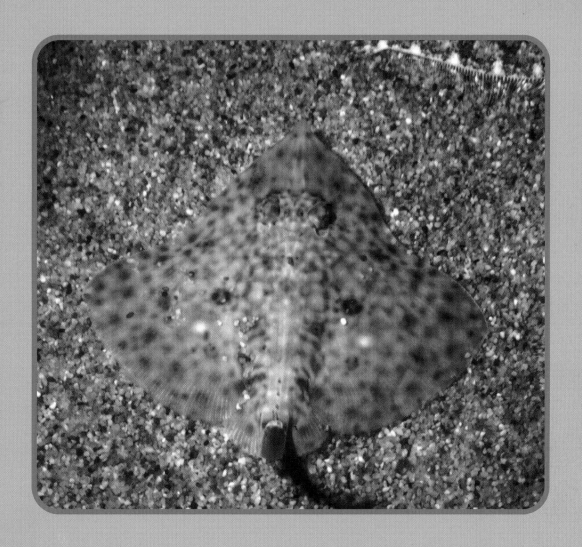

A shark can eat a **skate.** But the **eyespots** on the back of this skate will surprise a shark. A shark might leave the skate alone.

Who Is Hiding Here?

What animals are hiding here?
What kind of **camouflage** do they have?

For the answer, turn to page 19.

For the answer, turn to page 24.

Glossary

anemone   animal that lives on the ocean floor

alga (more than one are caled algae)   kind of small plant

camouflage   use of color, shape, or pattern to hide

countershading   top part of the animal is dark and the bottom part is light

cryptic coloration   colors that make an animal look like the place where it lives

disruptive coloration   pattern of colors on an animal that makes it hard to see the whole animal

eyespots   spots shaped like animal eyes that scare predators away

habitat   place where an animal or plant lives

microscope   tool used for looking at very small things. It makes small things look bigger.

mimic, mimicry   one animal looks and acts like a plant or another kind of animal

organ   part of an animal with a special purpose

pattern   colors arranged in shapes

poisonous   animal with a dangerous liquid inside of it

predator   animal that eats other animals

prey   animals that are eaten by other animals

skate   flat, round ocean animal related to sharks and rays

tentacle   part of an animal used for gripping

transparent   can see through

venomous   animal that puts a dangerous liquid into another animal

zooplankton   group of very small animals that live in the ocean

More Books to Read

Arnosky, Jim. *I See Animals Hiding.* New York: Scholastic, Incorporated, 2000.

Galko, Francine. *Sea Animals.* Chicago: Heinemann Library, 2002.

Kalman, Bobbie. *What Are Camouflage and Mimicry?* New York: Crabtree Publishing Company, 2001.

Index